Words of Love

Isobel Carlson

summersdale

WORDS OF LOVE
Copyright © Isobel Carlson 2009

Summersdale Publishers Ltd
46 West Street
Chichester
West Sussex
PO19 1RP
UK

www.summersdale.com

Printed and bound by Tien Wah Press, Singapore

ISBN: 978-1-84024-717-6

Words of Love

A collection of beautiful
poetry, prose and quotations

Isobel Carlson

To love and be loved is to feel the sun from both sides.

David Viscott

My bounty is as boundless as the sea, my
love as deep;
the more I give to thee, the more I have,
for both are infinite.

William Shakespeare,
Romeo and Juliet

Thou demandest what is Love. It is that powerful attraction towards all we conceive, or fear, or hope beyond ourselves, when we find within our own thoughts the chasm of an insufficient void, and seek to awaken in all things that are, a community with what we experience within ourselves. If we reason, we would be understood; if we imagine, we would that the airy children of our brain were born anew within another's; if we feel, we would that another's nerves should vibrate to our own, that the beams of their eyes should kindle at once and mix and melt into our own; that lips of motionless ice should not reply to lips quivering and burning with the heart's best blood. This is Love. This is the bond and the sanction which connects not only man with man, but with every thing which exists.

Percy Bysshe Shelley,
'On Love'

Lips and Eyes

In Celia's face a question did arise:
Which were more beautiful, her lips or eyes.
'We,' said the eyes, 'send forth those pointed darts
Which pierce the hardest adamantine hearts.'
'From us,' replied the lips, 'proceed those blisses
Which lovers reap by kind words and sweet kisses.'
Then wept the eyes, and from their springs did pour
Of liquid oriental pearl a shower,
Whereat the lips, moved with delight and pleasure,
Through a sweet smile unlocked their pearly treasure,
And bade Love judge whether did add more grace
Weeping or smiling pearls to Celia's face.

Thomas Carew

He was happy now, without a care in the world. A meal alone with her, a stroll along the highway in the evening, the way she touched her hand to her hair, the sight of her straw hat hanging from a window hasp, and many other things in which it had never occurred to him to look for pleasure – such now formed the steady current of his happiness.

Gustave Flaubert,
Madame Bovary

Friendship

A ruddy drop of manly blood
The surging sea outweighs;
The world uncertain comes and goes,
The lover rooted stays.
I fancied he was fled,
And, after many a year,
Glowed unexhausted kindliness,
Like daily sunrise there.

My careful heart was free again,
O friend, my bosom said,
Through thee alone the sky is arched,
Through thee the rose is red;
All things through thee take nobler form,
And look beyond the earth,
The mill-round of our fate appears
A sun-path in thy worth.
Me too thy nobleness has taught
To master my despair;
The fountains of my hidden life
Are through thy friendship fair.

Ralph Waldo Emerson,
Essays: First Series

There is only one happiness in life, to love and be loved.

George Sand

Sonnet

Let me not to the marriage of true minds
Admit impediments. Love is not love
Which alters when it alteration finds,
Or bends with the remover to remove:
O no! it is an ever-fixed mark,
That looks on tempests and is never shaken;
It is the star to every wandering bark,
Whose worth's unknown, although his height be taken.
Love's not Time's fool, though rosy lips and cheeks
Within his bending sickle's compass come:
Love alters not with his brief hours and weeks,
But bears it out even to the edge of doom.
If this be error and upon me prov'd,
I never writ, nor no man ever lov'd.

William Shakespeare

You will understand that I should like to say many fine and striking things to you, but it is rather difficult, all at once, in this way. I regret this all the more as you are sufficiently great to inspire one with romantic dreams of becoming the confidant of your beautiful soul...

*Marie Bashkirtseff
to Guy de Maupassant, 1884*

Sonnet

O my heart's heart and you who are to me
More than myself myself, God be with you,
Keep you in strong obedience, leal and true
To him whose noble service setteth free,
Give you all good we see or can foresee,
Make your joys many and your sorrows few,
Bless you in what you bear and what you do,
Yea, perfect you as He would have you be.
So much for you; but what for me dear friend?
To love you without stint and all I can
Today, tomorrow, world without an end:
To love you much, and yet to love you more,
As Jordan at its flood sweeps either shore;
Since woman is the helpmeet made for man.

Christina Rossetti

The Passionate Shepherd to His Love

Come live with me and be my love,
And we will all the pleasures prove
That valleys, groves, hills and fields,
Woods or steepy mountain yields.

And we will sit upon the rocks,
And see the shepherds feed their flocks
By shallow rivers, to whose falls
Melodious birds sing madrigals.

And I will make thee beds of roses
And a thousand fragrant posies;
A cap of flowers, and a kirtle
Embroidered all with leaves of myrtle.

A gown made of the finest wool
Which from our pretty lambs we pull;
Fair linèd slippers for the cold,
With buckles of the purest gold.

A belt of straw and ivy-buds
With coral clasps and amber studs:
And if these pleasures may thee move,
Come and live with me and be my love.

Thy shepherd swains shall dance and sing
For thy delight each May morning:
If these delights thy mind may move,
Then live with me and be my love.

Christopher Marlowe

You fear, sometimes, I do not love you so much as you wish? My dear girl I love you ever and ever and without reserve. The more I have known you the more have I lov'd. In every way – even my jealousies have been agonies of love, in the hottest fit I ever had I would have died for you.

The last of your kisses was ever the sweetest; the last smile the brightest; the last movement the gracefullest. When you pass'd my window home yesterday, I was fill'd with as much admiration as if I had then seen you for the first time.

John Keats
to Fanny Brawne, 1820

Where there is love there is no question.

Albert Einstein

The Exchange

We pledged our hearts, my love and I,
I in my arms the maiden clasping;
I could not tell the reason why,
But, O, I trembled like an aspen.

Her father's love she bade me gain;
I went, and shook like any reed!
I strove to act the man – in vain!
We had exchanged our hearts indeed.

Samuel Taylor Coleridge

The way you let your hand rest in mine, my bewitching sweetheart, fills me with happiness. It is the perfection of confiding love. Everything you do, the little unconscious things in particular, charms me and increases my sense of nearness to you, identification with you, till my heart is overflowing.

Woodrow Wilson

If I Were Loved, as I Desire to Be

If I were loved, as I desire to be,
What is there in the great sphere of the earth,
And range of evil between death and birth,
That I should fear – if I were loved by thee?
All the inner, all the outer world of pain
Clear Love would pierce and cleave, if thou wert mine,
As I have heard that, somewhere in the main,
Fresh-water springs come up through bitter brine.

'Twere joy, not fear, clasped hand in hand with thee,
To wait for death – mute – careless of all ills,
Apart upon a mountain, though the surge
Of some new deluge from a thousand hills
Flung leagues of roaring foam into the gorge
Below us, as far on as eye could see.

Alfred, Lord Tennyson

Life is a flower of which love is the honey.

Victor Hugo

Mr Bhaer saw the drops on her cheeks, though she turned her head away. The sight seemed to touch him very much, for suddenly stooping down, he asked in a tone that meant a great deal, 'Heart's dearest, why do you cry?'

Now, if Jo had not been new to this sort of thing she would have said she wasn't crying, had a cold in her head, or told any other feminine fib proper to the occasion. Instead of which, that undignified creature answered, with an irrepressible sob, 'Because you are going away.'

'*Ach, mein Gott*, that is so good!' cried Mr Bhaer, managing to clasp his hands in spite of the umbrella and the bundles, 'Jo, I haf nothing but much love to gif you. I came to see if you could care for it, and I waited to be sure that I was something more than a friend. Am I? Can you make a little place in your heart for old Fritz?' he added, all in one breath.

'Oh, yes!' said Jo, and he was quite satisfied, for she folded both hands over his arm, and looked up at him with an expression that plainly showed how happy she would be to walk through life beside him, even though she had no better shelter than the old umbrella, if he carried it.

Louisa May Alcott, Little Women

Sonnet

Shall I compare thee to a summer's day?
Thou art more lovely and more temperate:
Rough winds do shake the darling buds of May,
And summer's lease hath all too short a date:
Sometime too hot the eye of heaven shines,
And often is his gold complexion dimm'd;
And every fair from fair sometime declines,
By chance or nature's changing course untrimm'd;
But thy eternal summer shall not fade,
Nor lose possession of that fair thou ow'st;
Nor shall Death brag thou wander'st in his shade,
When in eternal lines to time thou grow'st;
So long as men can breathe, or eyes can see,
So long lives this, and this gives life to thee.

William Shakespeare

Eyes almost as deep and speaking he had seen before, and cheeks perhaps as fair... her mouth he had seen nothing to equal on the face of the earth. To a young man with the least fire in him that little upward lift in the middle of her red top lip was distracting, infatuating, maddening. He had never before seen a woman's lips and teeth which forced upon his mind with such persistent iteration the old Elizabethan simile of roses filled with snow. Perfect, he, as a lover, might have called them off-hand. But no – they were not perfect. And it was the touch of the imperfect upon the would-be perfect that gave the sweetness, because it was that which gave the humanity.

Thomas Hardy,
Tess of the D'Urbervilles

I Will Make You Brooches

I will make you brooches and toys for your delight
Of bird-song at morning and star-shine at night.
I will make a place fit for you and me
Of green days in forest and blue days at sea.

I will make my kitchen, and you shall keep your room,
Where white flows the river and bright blows the broom,
And you shall wash your linen and keep your body white
In rainfall at morning and dewfall at night.

And this shall be for music when no one else is near,
The fine song for singing, the rare song to hear!
That only I remember, that only you admire,
Of the broad road that stretches and the roadside fire.

Robert Louis Stevenson

Fragment 31

That man seems to me to be like a god, to
Sit so close to you and to hear your sweet voice
And your charming laughter – and all this, truly,
Makes my heart tremble;

For I only, briefly, need glance at you to
Find my voice has gone and my tongue is broken,
And a flame has stolen beneath my skin, my
Eyes can no longer

See, my ears are ringing, while drops of sweat run
Down my trembling body, and I've turned paler
Than a wisp of straw and it seems to me I'm
Not far off dying.

Sappho

I cannot exist without you – I am forgetful of everything but seeing you again – my life seems to stop there – I see no further. You have absorb'd me. I have a sensation at the present moment as though I were dissolving – I have been astonished that men could die martyrs for religion – I have shudder'd at it – I shudder no more – I could be martyr'd for my religion – Love is my religion – I could die for that – I could die for you. My creed is Love and you are its only tenet – You have ravish'd me away by a power I cannot resist.

John Keats

A Red Red Rose

O my Luve's like a red, red rose,
That's newly sprung in June;
O my Luve's like the melodie
That's sweetly play'd in tune.

As fair art thou, my bonie lass,
So deep in luve am I;
And I will love thee still, my Dear,
Till a' the seas gang dry.

Till a' the seas gang dry, my Dear,
And the rocks melt wi' the sun:
I will love thee still, my Dear,
While the sands o' life shall run.

And fare thee weel, my only Luve!
And fare thee weel, a while!
And I will come again, my Luve,
Tho' it were ten thousand mile!

Robert Burns

A life without love is like a year without summer.

Swedish Proverb

from The Anniversary

All other things to their destruction draw,
Only our love hath no decay;
This, no tomorrow hath, nor yesterday,
Running it never runs from us away,
But truly keeps his first, last, everlasting day.

John Donne

Love is patient, love is kind. It does not
envy, it does not boast, it is not proud. It
is not rude, it is not self-seeking, it is not
easily angered, it keeps no record of wrongs.
Love does not delight in evil but rejoices
with the truth. It always protects, always
trusts, always hopes, always perseveres.

Corinthians 13:4

Love is a canvas furnished by nature
and embroidered by imagination.

Voltaire

Elizabeth, feeling all the more than common awkwardness and anxiety of his situation, now forced herself to speak; and immediately, though not very fluently, gave him to understand that her sentiments had undergone so material a change, since the period to which he alluded, as to make her receive with gratitude and pleasure his present assurances. The happiness which this reply produced, was such as he had probably never felt before; and he expressed himself on the occasion as sensibly and as warmly as a man violently in love can be supposed to do. Had Elizabeth been able to encounter his eye, she might have seen how well the expression of heartfelt delight, diffused over his face, became him; but, though she could not look, she could listen, and he told her of feelings, which, in proving of what importance she was to him, made his affection every moment more valuable.

They walked on, without knowing in what direction. There was too much to be thought, and felt, and said, for attention to any other objects.

Jane Austen, *Pride and Prejudice*

First Love

I ne'er was struck before that hour
With love so sudden and so sweet;
Her face it bloomed like a sweet flower
And stole my heart away complete.
My face turned pale as deadly pale,
My legs refused to walk away,
And when she looked what could I ail?
My life and all seemed turned to clay.

And then my blood rushed to my face
And took my eyesight quite away;
The trees and bushes round the place
Seemed midnight at noonday.
I could not see a single thing,
Words from my eyes did start;
They spoke as chords do from the string
And blood burnt round my heart.

Are flowers the winter's choice?
Is love's bed always snow?
She seemed to hear my silent voice,
Not love's appeals to know.
I never saw so sweet a face
As that I stood before;
My heart has left its dwelling place
And can return no more.

John Clare

Through all Eternity to thee
A joyful song I'll raise,
For oh! Eternity's too short
To utter all thy Praise.

Joseph Addison

I have not spent a day without loving you;
I have not spent a night without embracing
you; I have not so much as drunk a cup of
tea without cursing the pride and ambition
which force me to remain separated from
the moving spirit of my life.

Napoleon Bonaparte to
Josephine Bonaparte, 1796

A kiss, when all is said, what is it?
An oath that's given closer than before;
A promise more precise; the sealing of
Confessions that till then were barely breathed;
A rosy dot placed on the i in loving;
A secret that is confined to a mouth and not to ears.

Edmond Rostand,
Cyrano de Bergerac

For a moment Anne's heart fluttered queerly and for the first time her eyes faltered under Gilbert's gaze and a rosy flush stained the paleness of her face. It was as if a veil that had hung before her inner consciousness had been lifted, giving to her view a revelation of unsuspected feelings and realities. Perhaps, after all, romance did not come into one's life with pomp and blare, like a gay knight riding down; perhaps it crept to one's side like an old friend through quiet ways; perhaps it revealed itself in seeming prose, until some sudden shaft of illumination flung athwart its pages betrayed the rhythm and the music, perhaps... perhaps... love unfolded naturally out of a beautiful friendship, as a golden-hearted rose slipping from its green sheath.

L. M. Montgomery,
Anne of Avonlea

So many contradictions, so many contrary movements are true, and can be explained in three words: I love you.

Julie de L'Espinasse to
Hippolyte de Guibert, 1774

To Helen

Helen, thy beauty is to me
Like those Nicèan barks of yore
That gently, o'er a perfumed sea
The weary way-worn wanderer bore
To his own native shore.

On desperate seas long wont to roam,
Thy hyacinth hair, thy classic face,
Thy Naiad airs have brought me home
To the glory that was Greece,
And the grandeur that was Rome.

Lo, in yon brilliant window-niche
How statue-like I see thee stand,
The agate lamp within thy hand,
Ah! Psyche, from the regions which
Are holy-land!

Edgar Allan Poe

April Love

We have walked in Love's land a little way
We have learnt his lesson a little while,
And shall we not part at the end of day,
With a sigh, a smile?

A little while in the shine of the sun,
We were twined together, joined lips forgot
How the shadows fall when the day is done,
And when Love is not.

We have made no vows – there will none be broke,
Our love was free as the wind on the hill,
There was no word said we need wish unspoke,
We have wrought no ill.

So shall we not part at the end of day,
Who have loved and lingered a little while,
Join lips for the last time, go our way,
With a sigh, a smile.

Ernest Dowson

If you only knew how much I love you, how essential you are to my life, you would not dare stay away for an instant, you would always remain pressed close to my heart, your soul to my soul.

Juliette Drouet to Victor Hugo, 1833

My love for Linton is like the foliage in the woods: time will change it, I'm well aware, as winter changes the trees. My love for Heathcliff resembles the eternal rocks beneath: a source of little visible delight, but necessary. Nelly, I am Heathcliff! He's always, always in my mind: not as a pleasure, any more than I am always a pleasure to myself, but as my own being.

Emily Brontë,
Wuthering Heights

The Garden of Beauty

Coming to kiss her lips (such grace I found),
Me seem'd I smelt a garden of sweet flow'rs
That dainty odours from them threw around,
For damsels fit to deck their lovers' bow'rs.
Her lips did smell like unto gilliflowers,
Her ruddy cheeks like unto roses red,
Her snowy brows like budded bellamoures,
Her lovely eyes like pinks but newly spread,
Her goodly bosom like a strawberry bed,
Her neck like to a bunch of cullambines,
Her breast like lilies ere their leaves be shed,
Her nipples like young blossom'd jessamines:
Such fragrant flow'rs do give most odourous smell,
But her sweet odour did them all excel.

Edmund Spenser

Love does not consist in gazing at each other but in looking in the same direction.

Antoine de Saint-Exupéry

His arms were fast around her, he seemed to be gathering her into himself, her warmth, her softness, her adorable weight, drinking in the suffusion of her physical being, avidly. He lifted her, and seemed to pour her into himself, like wine into a cup... How perfect and foreign he was – ah, how dangerous! Her soul thrilled with complete knowledge. This was the glistening forbidden apple, this face of a man. She kissed him, putting her fingers over his face, his eyes, his nostrils, over his brows and his ears, to his neck, to know him, to gather him in by touch.

D. H. Lawrence, Women in Love

All love, at first, like generous wine,
Ferments and frets until 'tis fine,
But, when 'tis settled on the lee,
And from th' impurer matter free,
Becomes the richer still the older,
And proves the pleasanter the colder.

Samuel Butler

I Love Thee

I love thee – I love thee!
'Tis all that I can say;
It is my vision in the night,
My dreaming in the day;
The very echo of my heart,
The blessing when I pray.
I love thee – I love thee!

I love thee – I love thee!
Is ever on my tongue.
In all my proudest poesy
That chorus still is sung;
It is the verdict of my eyes
Amidst the gay and young:
I love thee – I love thee!
A thousand maids among.

I love thee – I love thee!
Thy bright and hazel glance,
The mellow lute upon those lips,
Whose tender tones entrance.
But most dear heart of hearts, thy proofs.
That still these words enhance!
I love thee – I love thee!
Whatever be thy chance.

Thomas Hood

I can listen no longer in silence. I must speak to you by such means as are within my reach. You pierce my soul. I am half agony, half hope. Tell me not that I am too late, that such precious feelings are gone for ever. I offer myself to you again with a heart even more your own than when you almost broke it, eight years and a half ago. Dare not say that man forgets sooner than woman, that his love has an earlier death. I have loved none but you. Unjust I may have been, weak and resentful I have been, but never inconstant. You alone have brought me to Bath. For you alone, I think and plan. Have you not seen this? Can you fail to have understood my wishes? I had not waited even these ten days, could I have read your feelings, as I think you must have penetrated mine. I can hardly write. I am every instant hearing something which overpowers me. You sink your voice, but I can distinguish the tones of that voice when they would be lost on others. Too good, too excellent creature! You do us justice, indeed. You do believe that there is true attachment and constancy among men. Believe it to be most fervent, most undeviating...

Jane Austen, *Persuasion*

Love is something eternal; the aspect
may change, but not the essence.

Vincent van Gogh

... there came a vivid flash of lightning which lit each of them up for the other – and the light seemed to be the terror of a hopeless love. Dorothea darted instantaneously from the window; Will followed her, seizing her hand with a spasmodic movement; and so they stood, with their hands clasped, like two children, looking out on the storm, while the thunder gave a tremendous crack and roll above them, and the rain began to pour down. Then they turned their faces towards each other, with the memory of his last words in them, and they did not loose each other's hands.

George Eliot, Middlemarch

I Love My Love in the Morning

I love my love in the morning,
For she like morn is fair –
Her blushing cheek, its crimson streak,
It clouds her golden hair.
Her glance, its beam, so soft and kind;
Her tears, its dewy showers;
And her voice, the tender whispering wind
That stirs the early bowers.

I love my love in the morning,
I love my love at noon,
For she is bright as the lord of light,
Yet mild as autumn's moon:
Her beauty is my bosom's sun
Her faith my fostering shade,
And I will love my darling one,
Till even the sun shall fade.

I love my love in the morning,
I love my love at even;
Her smile's soft play is like the ray
That lights the western heaven:
I loved her when the sun was high,
I loved her when he rose;
But best of all when evening's sigh
Was murmuring at its close.

Gerald Griffin

Come, O Come

Come, O come, my life's delight,
Let me not in languor pine!
Love loves no delay; thy sight,
The more enjoyed, the more divine:
O come, and take from me
The pain of being deprived of thee!

Thou all sweetness dost enclose,
Like a little world of bliss.

Beauty guards thy looks: the rose
In them pure and eternal is.
Come, then, and make thy flight
As swift to me, as heavenly light.

Thomas Campion

Can no honest man have a prepo[sse]ssion for a fine woman, but he must run his head against an intrigue? Take a little of the tender witchcraft of Love, and add it to the generous, the honorable sentiments of manly friendship, and I know but one more friendly morsel, which few, few in any rank ever taste. Such a composition is like adding cream to the strawberries: it not only gives the fruit a more elegant richness, but has a peculiar deliciousness of its own.

*Robert Burns to Clarinda
(Agnes MacLehose), 1787*

Poem 5

Lesbia, live with me and love me
So we'll laugh at all the sour-faced
Strictures of the wise.
This sun once set will rise again,
When our sun sets
Follows night and an endless sleep.
Kiss me now a thousand times
And now a hundred more
And then a hundred
And then a thousand more again,
Till with so many hundred thousand
Kisses you and I shall both lose count
Nor any can from envy of
So much kissing
Put his finger on the number
Of sweet kisses you of me
And I of you, darling, have had.

Catullus

But to see her was to love her, love but her, and love her forever.

Robert Burns

To Ellen

Oh! might I kiss those eyes of fire,
A million scarce would quench desire:
Still would I steep my lips in bliss,
And dwell an age on every kiss;
Nor then my soul should sated be,
Still would I kiss and cling to thee:
Nought should my kiss from thine dissever;
Still would we kiss, and kiss forever,
E'en though the numbers did exceed
The yellow harvest's countless seed.
To part would be a vain endeavor:
Could I desist? Ah, never-never!

Lord Byron

Dearest, – I wish I had the gift of making rhymes, for methinks there is poetry in my head and heart since I have been in love with you. You are a poem. You are a sort of sweet, simple, gay, pathetic ballad, which Nature is singing, sometimes with tears, sometimes with smiles, and sometimes intermingled smiles and tears.

*Nathaniel Hawthorne
to Sophie Hawthorne, 1839*

Was this the face that launched a thousand ships
and burnt the topless towers of Ilium?
Sweet Helen, make me immortal with a kiss.
Her lips suck forth my soul – see where it flies!
Come, Helen, come, give me my soul again.
Here will I dwell, for heaven is in these lips
And all is dross that is not Helena.
I will be Paris, and for love of thee
Instead of Troy, shall Wittenberg be sack'd,
And I will combat with weak Menelaus,

And wear thy colours on my plumèd crest;
Yea, I will wound Achillies in the heel,
And then return to Helen for a kiss.
O thou art fairer than the evening air
Clad in the beauty of a thousand stars!
Brighter art thou than flaming Jupiter,
When he appear'd to hapless Semele,
More lovely than the monarch of the sky
In wanton Arethusa's azur'd arms,
And none but thou shalt be my paramour!

Christopher Marlowe, Doctor Faustus

Having once set out, and felt that he had done so, on this road to happiness, there was nothing on the side of prudence to stop him or make his progress slow; no doubts of her deserving, no fears of opposition of taste, no need of drawing new hopes of happiness from dissimilarity of temper. Her mind, disposition, opinions, and habits wanted no half concealment, no self-deception on the present, no reliance on future improvement. Even in the midst of his late infatuation, he had acknowledged Fanny's mental superiority. What must be his sense of it now, therefore? She was of course only too good for him; but as nobody minds having what is too good for them, he was very steadily earnest in the pursuit of the blessing, and it was not possible that encouragement from her should be long wanting. Timid, anxious, doubting as she was, it was still impossible that such tenderness as hers should not, at times, hold out the strongest hope of success, though it remained for a later period to tell him the whole delightful and astonishing truth. His happiness in knowing himself to have been so long the beloved of such a heart, must have been great enough to warrant any strength of language in which he could clothe it to her or to himself; it must have been a delightful happiness. But there was happiness elsewhere which no description can reach. Let no one presume to give the feelings of a young woman on receiving the assurance of that affection of which she has scarcely allowed herself to entertain a hope.

Jane Austen, *Mansfield Park*

Then seek not, sweet, the 'If' and 'Why' I love you now until I die.

Christopher Brennan

My heart overflows with emotion and joy!
I do not know what heavenly languor, what
infinite pleasure permeates it and burns me
up. It is as if I had never loved!!! Tell me
whence these uncanny disturbances springs,
these inexpressible foretastes of delight,
these divine tremors of love.

Franz Liszt to Marie d'Agoult, 1834

Love and the Rose

The rose is fairest when 'tis budding new,
And hope is brightest when it dawns from fears:
The rose is sweetest wash'd with morning dew,
And love is loveliest when embalm'd in tears.
O wilding rose, whom fancy thus endears,
I bid your blossoms in my bonnet wave,
Emblem of hope and love through future years!
Thus spoke young Norman, heir of Armandare
What time the sun arose on Vennachar's broad wave.

Sir Walter Scott

In such inadequate language my feelings struggled for expression they could not get it; speech, brittle and unmalleable, and cold as ice, dissolved or shivered in the effort. He watched me still: he gently raised his hand to stroke my hair; it touched my lips in passing; I pressed it close, I paid it tribute. He was my king; royal for me had been that hand's bounty; to offer homage was both a joy and a duty.

Charlotte Brontë, *Villette*

The Marriage Ring

The ring, so worn as you behold,
So thin, so pale, is yet of gold:
The passion such it was to prove –
Worn with life's care, love yet was love.

George Crabbe

Love is... born with the pleasure of looking at each other, it is fed with the necessity of seeing each other, it is concluded with the impossibility of separation.

José Martí y Pérez

The Nymph's Reply to the Shepherd

If all the world and love were young,
And truth in every shepherd's tongue,
These pretty pleasures might me move
To live with thee and be thy love.

But Time drives flocks from field to fold;
When rivers rage and rocks grow cold;
And Philomel becometh dumb;
The rest complains of cares to come.

The flowers do fade, and wanton fields
To wayward Winter reckoning yields:
A honey tongue, a heart of gall,
Is fancy's spring, but sorrow's fall.

Thy gowns, thy shoes, thy beds of roses,
Thy cap, thy kirtle, and thy posies,
Soon break, soon wither, soon forgotten –
In folly ripe, in reason rotten.

Thy belt of straw and ivy – buds,
Thy coral clasps and amber studs –
All these in me no means can move
To come to thee and be thy love.

But could youth last, and love still breed,
Had joys no date, nor age no need,
Then these delights my mind might move
To live with thee and be thy love.

Sir Walter Raleigh

Sonnet

My lady's presence makes the roses red
Because to see her lips they blush for shame;
The lily's leaves, for envy, pale became,
For her white hands in them this envy bred.
The marigold the leaves abroad doth spread,
Because the sun's and her power is the same
The violet of purple colour came,
Dyed in the blood she made my heart to shed.
In brief, all flowers from her their virtue take;
From her sweet breath their sweet smells do proceed;
The living heat which her eyebeams do make
Warmeth the ground, and quickeneth the seed.
The rain, wherewith she watereth the flowers,
Falls from mine eyes, which she dissolves in showers.

Henry Constable

You know I would with pleasure give up all here and all beyond the grave for you, and in refraining from this, must my motives be misunderstood?

I was and am yours freely and most entirely, to obey, to honour, love – and fly with you when, where, and how you yourself might and may determine.

Lord Byron to
Lady Caroline Lambe, 1812

I

All nature blooms when you appear;
The fields their richest liv'ries wear;
Oaks, elms and pines, blest with your view,
Shoot out fresh greens, and bud anew;
  The varying seasons you supply;
  And when you're gone, they fade and die.

II

Sweet Philomel, in mournful strains,
To you appeals, to you complains.
The tow'ring lark, on rising wing,
Your praise, delighted, seems to sing;
  Presaging, as aloft he flies,
  Your future progress through the skies.

III

The purple violet, damask rose,
Each, to delight your senses, blows.
The lilies ope', as you appear;
And all the beauties of the year
    Diffuse their odours at your feet,
    Who give to ev'ry flow'r its sweet.

IV

For flow'rs and women are allied;
Both Nature's glory, and her pride!
Of ev'ry fragrant sweet possest,
They bloom but for the fair-one's breast;
    And to the swelling bosom borne,
    Each other mutually adorn.

Samuel Richardson, Pamela

How do I love thee? Let me count the ways.
I love thee to the depth and breadth and height
My soul can reach, when feeling out of sight
For the ends of Being and ideal Grace.
I love thee to the level of every day's
Most quiet need, by sun and candlelight.
I love thee freely, as men strive for Right;
I love thee purely, as they turn from Praise.
I love thee with the passion put to use
In my old griefs, and with my childhood's faith.
I love thee with a love I seemed to lose
With my lost saints, – I love thee with the breath,
Smiles, tears, of all my life! – and, if God choose,
I shall but love thee better after death.

Elizabeth Barrett Browning,
Sonnets from the Portuguese

But if you wish me to love you, could you but see how much I *do* love you, you would be proud and content. All my heart is yours, sir: it belongs to you; and with you it would remain, were fate to exile the rest of me from your presence forever.

Charlotte Brontë, *Jane Eyre*

If I know what love is, it is because of you.

Herman Hesse

Love's Philosophy

The fountains mingle with the river
And the rivers with the Ocean,
The winds of Heaven mix for ever
With a sweet emotion;
Nothing in the world is single;
All things by a law divine
In one spirit meet and mingle.
Why not I with thine? –

See the mountains kiss high Heaven
And the waves clasp one another;
No sister-flower would be forgiven
If it disdained its brother;
And the sunlight clasps the earth
And the moonbeams kiss the sea:
What is all this sweet work worth
If thou kiss not me?

Percy Bysshe Shelley

She Walks in Beauty

She walks in Beauty, like the night
Of cloudless climes and starry skies;
And all that's best of dark and bright
Meet in her aspect and her eyes:
Thus mellowed to that tender light
Which heaven to gaudy day denies.

One shade the more, one ray the less,
Had half impaired the nameless grace
Which waves in every raven tress,
Or softly lightens o'er her face;
Where thoughts serenely sweet express
How pure, how dear their dwelling place.

And on that cheek, and o'er that brow,
So soft, so calm, yet eloquent,
The smiles that win, the tints that glow,
But tell of days in goodness spent,
A mind at peace with all below,
A heart whose love is innocent!

Lord Byron

The count shuddered at the tone of this voice, which awoke the deepest fibres of his being. His eyes met those of the young woman and could not bear to look into them. 'My God, my God!' he said. 'Can what you hinted to me be true? Haydée, would you be happy then not to leave me?'

'I am young,' she answered softly. 'I love life, which you have always made so pleasant for me. I should be sorry to die.'

'Do you mean that if I were to leave you, Haydée...'

'Yes, my Lord, I should die!'

'Do you love me, then?'

'Oh, Valentine, he asks if I love him! Tell him: do you love Maximilien?'

The count felt his breast swell and his heart fill. He opened his arms and Haydée threw herself into them with a cry. 'Oh, yes! Oh, yes I love you!' she said. 'I love you as one loves a father, a brother, a husband! I love you as one loves life, and loves God, for you are to me the most beautiful, the best and greatest of created beings!'

'Let it be as you will, my sweet angel!' said the count. 'God, who roused me against my enemies and gave me great victory, God, I can see, does not wish my victory to end with that regret. I wished to punish myself, but God wants to pardon me. So, love me, Haydée! Who knows? Perhaps your love will make me forget what I have to forget.'

Alexandre Dumas,
The Count of Monte Cristo

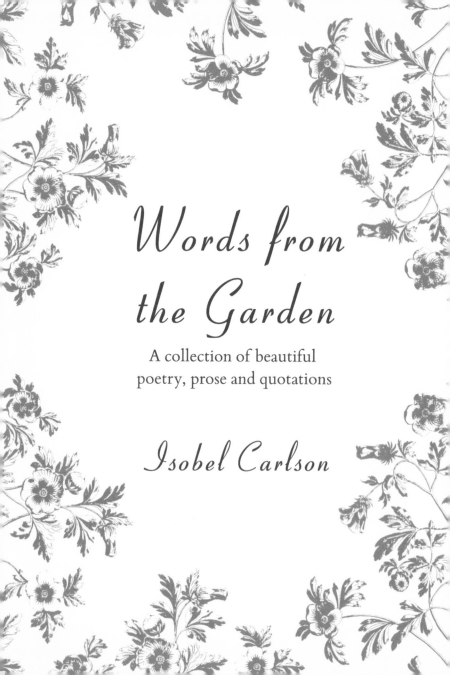

Words from the Garden

A collection of beautiful
poetry, prose and quotations

Isobel Carlson

Words from the Garden

A collection of beautiful poetry, prose and quotations

Isobel Carlson

ISBN: 978 1 84024 653 7   Hardback   £6.99

'*This charming hardback book would be best read outdoors on a sunny Sunday afternoon, accompanied by the noises of nature…*'
CONCEPT FOR LIVING Magazine

'*A collection of beautiful poetry, prose and quotations – all with a garden theme*'   WESTON & WORLE NEWS

'*plenty of evocative poetry, prose and quotations in a pocket-sized book… sure to be cherished by all garden lovers*'
NORTH DEVON JOURNAL

Garden lovers everywhere will cherish this collection of poetry and prose inspired by all things green and flourishing. With quotations from down the ages and through the seasons, this beautiful book contains words of wisdom on everything from allotments to arboretums, from pergolas to potting sheds, and will provide moments of laughter and reflection whether you are cooped up on a rainy day or admiring the fruits of your labour on a summer evening.

www.summersdale.com